# BLOODHOUND

*A Poetry Collection*

Marie Casey

for all those
masking the scent
of their blood

# THE BEGINNING

The evening I came back in that unexpected gunfire and pile of feces, I had emerged from the depths of gray matter. I could see the surprise on your face. It was hard not to admire your blushed cheeks, the way your mouth drooped ever so slightly open. The horror in your eyes, it danced. It's like you had seen a ghost or fire. Perhaps? No? Well, maybe you were shocked to see a vampire walking around in the daylight. Such a silly girl. There was nothing stardust could do for you.

Even after all we had been through, I would've still let you use my sorrows to strengthen your cup of tea for only a glimmer of a smile. Those first moments back, I craved nothing more than the sight of your fangs, as I am sure they were still stained with my blood, with bits of flesh stuck in between the gums. Your skin gleamed from your consumption of blood, it hummed with my essence. You see, I had been alive in your capillaries for years. I haunted your innards. That nausea that you felt under the fluorescent lights, that was me.

I was digging my way out, but you were a stubborn individual. You buried me so far down it took nearly a decade for me to find my way out of the desolation.

I hope my initial presence brought you discomfort, caused more damage than the claw mark indentations I left behind as my blood loss spiraled from a dribble to a hemorrhage. I exposed much more than my skin, but even with the shedding of my epidermis, you let my arteries pump dry. Nothing was enough. You demanded soul, dedication, but I was prepared to give this to you! Dirty games, confused lies. No matter what I did, how much blood I poured, it never pleased you. I know this now, which is why I cherish that agonized expression as I emerged.

Petty, I know, but after ten years, thoughts of you linger within my shell. It's maddening. Rejection doesn't fade, just lives inside various compartments of the brain. Most days I don't access them. It comes out in the strangest and most unexpected moments, like when I see a yellow balloon, remember? Perhaps not, you were never fond of my offerings. Ungrateful from the beginning.

What about the grocery store? You must remember where we met. How you stood out in a sea of uniforms. Those horrible polyester polos and ill-fitting pants. But nothing, not even societal expectations, could have dimmed your light. I loved how you burned my skin. And after all these years, I can't remove the burn marks.

I never forgot the sensation of your breath, the partial shutdown of my frontal lobe, the blood flow to particular places. It's those eyes. That smile. You remember you used to smile at me, right? It wasn't always a horror story in a sprawl. The baring of teeth started all of this. Those fangs. You'd wave and smile as I walked by. I felt more like a human then, of course. I'd come to life as you hummed my name. I don't know if you knew, but it induced heart murmurs and temporary lung failure. And for as painful as it sounds, I'd do anything for that feeling again. It's funny how questioning organ failure could make me feel so alive.

We had this whimsical connection of threads and spikes, many of which still link us together. I can't explain it. I know you can't either. It's not something other people will understand, too taboo. And no matter what you do, don't lie and say you didn't feel it either. It was there, especially in the beginning.

What are you waiting for?
Rip open those ventricles
and tell me your story.

My capillaries defy all odds
as I burden them with cigarette smoke,
constricting their capacity to pump blood,
allowing my organs to suffocate.

But, with your footsteps,
my blood pressure spikes,
supplying enough oxygen to my lungs
to stutter hello.

Be wary of the allure,
as my depths are hollow,
words will reverberate
festering whimsical ideologies,
tormenting the frontal lobe
in pursuit to furnish
a concave of desolation.

Let's run hand in hand
amongst the wooden giants,
stepping on puffballs.

Through the black clouds,
we will lift our veils,
shedding our cadavers,
finding vitality in each other.

Intoxicating smoke
billows out of control
as I take a safety pin
to tighten up my bra.
I have hopes you'd look
and know I do this for you,
but through the smoke,
you will discover
how despondent I am
to avoid being alone.

Moments of inclusion
emerge in the starlight,
dim, complex networks.
With the rise of the sun,
weak strands confess,
brisk wildfires depopulate.
A disenchanting freedom disentangles,
the persistent tie to the stain on the wall.

look into the iris,
see the swirls,
blue and yellow,
a galaxy
waiting for study,
eager to let you in
but, with hesitant feet,
protection can be granted
from the gaping black hole.

Bare witness to my awkwardness.
It's unexpected as I cover it with locks,
articulating wisdom in short spurts.
But corner me, words will trip and tumble
and as I try to catch my breath
your eyes will roll so far back into your head
I'll be forced to climb
through your fibrous membranes
only to regain an ounce of my lost self-respect.

When biting my nails,
I have no restraint.
My heartbeat ruptures
leaking throughout my body.
And sometimes, when I bite too much,
the blood dribbles out,
but I don't let anyone see.
I am collecting it in vials
in the hope to conjure a soul
that will ail me from slaughter.

Let's not pretend there weren't cravings,
in fact, I was famished.
A lifetime of neglected nourishment
then you strolled along,
found yourself inside my pores,
and it consumed my endocrine system.
I relished in your sweaty reactions;
tight jeans, pushup bra, swaying hips,
how high you'd jump for a moment.
And in the beginning,
I had more control than you,
it's funny how that works.
But I wonder if that's what fueled the fire
because what I thought was fun,
turned into an inferno,
that would burn me alive.

# INSIDIOUS INTENTIONS

Oh, dear. Blurred stems are hard to see in the dark, but there is always an excitement of blooming flowers with or without sight. Spring has that way about it. I think it's the smell, the sweetest of smells, especially after the rain. Perhaps you thought we were in another season? I can accept having differing perceptions of the darkness. That what blurred for me did not blur for you, and I suppose flowers do die in the fall, those springtime feelings can't last forever. And for as much as I was attracted to your pollen, I cannot deny your cruel winds. Frost spewed from your lips, even in the changing of seasons. All I could do was add more layers to my wardrobe. Which I always did, for you.

When my petals began to shrivel, I dug myself some holes. I could sense your discomfort and wanted to elongate my inevitable fall. Did you know how much it took to approach you? Perhaps that wasn't it, maybe you gave yourself chills. I saw your scleras ice over. And through the fog, I could always see your eyes turn the other way in my presence. That's when the blood started draining. Could you smell it? The blood?

I hid, masked my scent in the shadows. I had hoped my wounds would heal out of your view. No need for you to have seen such awful sights. And I suppose I knew I lacked powers of foresight as I kept bleeding and it always shocked me. With each side-eye shutter and ignoring acknowledgment, the paler I became. My intentions were not insidious, I was curious, exploring our elaborate web. You demonized my exploration and look at me now! I'm nothing more than what you wanted me to be. Desperate for blood. Your speculation blossomed in realism. Clairvoyance of a festering enchantress.

But, again, I lingered, for you. Whenever you'd be ready. We could fall into any hole you desired, intertwine our roots and let them grow beneath the surface. It's all I ever wanted. I endured the gashes and wreckage for you. Why don't you believe me? Why do you tell another story?

My skin struggles to absorb the sunlight.
So, I take a supplement of vitamin D,
it suffices, but it's not the same.
Synthetic nourishment,
not unlike your intentions.

I know you can see me,
you have sight that requires
more than eyes.

You may be the only one.

I've transpired,
living past my expiration date,
which was preventable
as all I needed to stay fresh
was what you had offered.

But how you decided to deliver,
rotted out my core,
and I decayed inside cellophane.

And now, I can't move
without concaving inwards.

let me
rip out
your sternum
and see
what
you're
protecting

Fold me like paper,
whatever shape you desire.
Shredded?
Licentious?
Fairy wings?
It's your choice,
as my only defense is a papercut,
which heals fast
and is easily forgotten.

Glittery appeal
draws me in.
Playful dances.
Joyful moments.
Yet, a rotten stench
clogs the air
as my nostril hairs burn,
the sparkles vanish
and fire appears.

napping in the wild,
fabrications emit bliss,
seeping from my neurons,
broadcasting unfulfillment
to a personal audience
constructed inside my head.

I took a trip to space
to see the stardust.
Charmed,

how the elements
harmonized with mine.
Bewitched,

intertwining swirls,
providing solace amongst the stars,
enticing me to embrace.

I allow for modifications.
It's no ordeal,
I'll breathe another day.

Unaware of the full metamorphosis,
taking place under the surface,
that will remove my helmet

making it impossible to breathe.

Elegant lace drapes over the fireplace,
impenetrable to the flame,
the lace remains
see-through and vain.

I saw you today.
I hid behind an endcap.
I watched you hunt in aisles.
I couldn't tell if it was in my head.
You were searching for something.
Someone.
Was it all in my head?
Or were you looking for me?

Underneath the smile,
the kind eyes,
that feeling that made me
worthwhile,
lived your
insidious intentions.

I stand in line,
guard down, ready to buy.

I chat with a friend
blissful, in laughter,
enjoying mediocrity
as much as we can.

Waiting our turn,
I feel a tapping,
pressure on my shoulder.

So, I turn around
and there you were
grinning with unlikely coincidence
of such extraordinary circumstances
that we meet in the same line
over and over again
as if the stars have aligned
to ensure a guided path
for you to find me
without even trying.

# BLOODHOUND

I've waited, taken mortal wounds, stained the carpet everywhere I walked. It was all a plea to get noticed. It was sad, pathetic, I'm aware. But there was little I wouldn't have done to see that sparkle in your eyes, like in the beginning, when we'd talk outside. Dear, did you ever see me beyond that picnic table? I could never figure that out. You always seemed so unfazed, disinterested. Sometimes you blatantly did not respond. I offered you whatever you wanted, but part of me thought you liked to see me bleed.

Then you stopped going out, limiting your public appearances. It was as though you feared the sunlight. You were rarely alone, and when you did expose yourself to the elements, I'd have to track your scent in a crowd. I hated it when I'd have to greet you with other people around. They took away your energy; you acted differently. Smug, detached. But I knew you weren't really like that. Remember how I could read your soul? How I could smell your blood as soon as you entered a room. It was an act for your friends, I knew you better than that. I watched you long enough to know.

I had minimal options left at my fingertips, but I remained patient. I let the clock hands rotate far more than should have been necessary. I thought that's what you needed to catch onto my scent. Yet, I grew weary of each passing season, I could only wait so long before I couldn't. It started innocently with that yellow balloon on your front lawn. I just wanted to celebrate another year of your existence. For you to know I would share that celebration with you. You never thanked me for that, did you know? One of the few people capable of seeing through the layers of your bark, to smell what filled your branches, and you tossed me in a gutter with your leaves. Unbelievable.

Eventually, I couldn't help myself. I'd go for drives to catch a glimpse. And how you loved to keep your windows open. Late night dances with the stars. Your dust swirling around, wrapped in only a towel. There was little in my power to look away, and I didn't. I wanted to tell you, and when I did, it was the first time I died. When you closed the window and shut me out, my heart stopped. From then on I followed like a bloodhound addicted to your scent. And as I said, you gave me no other option and I could not get you out of my nostrils.

flashes inside my head,
mutilated limbs,
carnal bits,
opera songs,
it's enough to go catatonic,
just until i'm convinced it's not real.

Uncover the light,
expose shameful weaknesses,
mortal contaminates
sporing in my brainstem,
but I have accepted eradication as
unperceivable;
a blight I must endure alone
as I have inflicted it upon myself.
It pollutes my energy,
misaligning my chakras
and weakens my soul.

It's all because
I could not raise my voice
while yours boomed,
reverberating down my throat
and unleashing the toxins
trapped on my tungsten wire.

enjoy the touch,
take in the smells,
revel in your emotions,
as i shut down
closing off entry,
building a fortress
so tall, so impenetrable
acquiring access
remains unknown.

covering tracks,
dirt and soot,
body scrub made of bark,
tea tree oils,
altering scents,
no deterrents deter
bloodhound noses
as they smell much more
than pheromones.

No, not today.

There's a blockade,
blanketed by patterns,
cushioning the strain.

Little can filter through.

But the chambers are overflowing,
abusing the lining,
deteriorating the gray matter,
sending surges of chemicals
in a plea for release.

Only to be ignored
and saved for another day.

i want it back,
you removed it
without permission,
undetermined of your awareness
of my idle status,
awaiting for instruction
to determine
my next move
even though what was stolen
has never been tangible enough to possess,
a mere delusion I constructed
as you pillaged me
of all things
that gave me the sensation
of fortifiable protection.

I was wary of the dark
before I met you,
but now
I'm even suspicious
of shadows.

It wasn't the hunt
or the what ifs
or the when ifs
or the how ifs
that drove me frenetic,
had my pores crying,
it was what occurred behind closed doors
that was self-inflicted.
As you see, the only way to purge
was to beat it out of me
with brutal remarks and crippling distortions
because maybe why you followed me
was something that I caused.
Maybe this whole thing was all my fault.

# HEMORRHAGE

I know you saw me, you ungrateful child. I placed optimism and dreams in a bag and hand-fed them to you. Every piece of candy in the store. I baked your name into cookies and pies. Any sugary substance to get your mouth to salivate and I pleaded then as I do now, why? Can you at least tell me why? What the hell could you have wanted that I did not already feed you? I had offered emotional bonds, monetary sacrifices, and mind altering substances. Anything to entice you. Could you see how desperate I was? Did you enjoy the show?

I think you did. I think you were tripping on power, laughing it up with your peers. I saw the peeks and giggles as I walked by, the ever so slight dips, pretending you didn't jump in nude. Do you think I am blind? Or stupid? Connection and consideration was all I asked. Was that really so terrible? Must be some kind of crime against nature, right? I suppose your nature.

I could sense you were as lonely as I was, still am. People like us can smell the desolation in others, it's in the blood. And your eyes betrayed you from the start. No matter how many people surrounded you, your eyes remained the same. Forlorn. Longing to be witnessed. But I screamed at the stars to tell them that I did. I saw you, did they tell you? I think they forgot because soon after you gaped into a wild black hole which I could not control.

You didn't care, consumed as you pleased, and vomited out the rest. And I started to have these days where I didn't want to think about you. I didn't want to have to deal with your flat affect and sheepish tease. Sometimes, I succeeded and all my troubles evaporated into the glass jar where I lived. But the bliss always dissipated as the condensation built up around the rim and would drip into my eyes. They still burn, my eyes.

And if I had any blood left, it would boil in my memories, always remaining too bitter to swallow. Watching me suffer tighten your core, brighten your smile. That's why I told people things about you. Things we may or may not have done together. It's all I had, do you understand me? You stripped me of any kind of power. And because of you, I exposed my fantasies to the world. Things I wanted to share with you, but you wouldn't let me. I was losing your scent, and I needed you to bleed to find it again.

Tick, tick, tick.
Do you hear it?
The sound of the bomb
slowly erupting?
Have no fear missing this spectacle
as the explosion will last for years.

I have these moments
where I want to tear off heads,
bathe in blood,
exfoliate my skin,
for, I've been triggered,
and it accentuates all the hatred
festering inside my claws.

grab a spoon,
a bag of crackers,
my heart is in a boil
cooked with liver and tripe,
the smell is atrocious
and too hot to swallow,
but i beg you to sit down
and enjoy the soup
and scald your throat out on me.

An aggravated chronicle,
tacit intentions rupture.

The veins leak,
contaminated blood
spreads through reflection
plaguing the spirit.

It's going to scratch my throat out,
no matter how much I rub my head
or distort my hands.
The quiver in my lip
will become a howl to the moon,
only to be skewed in misinterpretation
of barks and whimpers,
ignoring the elephant with talons
standing on my chest.

No, sage won't do,
I'll need an ice pick to
scramble my brains
to escape from you.

Don't touch it,
it's ready to burst
and with any pressure,
it's sure to rupture,
splattering on the walls.

I've lost control.

So, don't acknowledge it,
pretend it doesn't exist,
because it can't open
without hemorrhaging.

It's funny,
no matter how often
I smash my fists
into the wall,
no blood comes out.

I can't describe the substance
clogging my throat.
I try to swallow,
but the goo latches to my vocal cords.
I try to scream,
but I can't make myself heard.
I try stabbing a hollow pen in my trachea,
but the blood makes me gurgle.
So, I grab a bottle and chug
to flood the pathways,
in hopes that my subconscious will escape.
A solution for my clog,
but it releases the flames.

Anger can't describe how I feel,
it's an emotion much more powerful.
Rage?
Wrath?
Vexation?
None suffice,
as it cannot be conceptualized in one feeling.

Rather it's a bitter brew stewing in a cauldron,
bubbling at the surface, splashing,
staining the walls with unpleasant odors,
a lucid reminder of defiled dreams
never available for ingestion.

So, I join the witches in their rituals,
drinking their potions
in order to mourn the life
that never came to be.

# DRAINED

The only thing I could do was snicker as I was depleted of blood, and I finally got my turn to watch you spiral down the drain. I watched as you slept in bathtubs praying for rising waters to wash you away. I hoped you'd drowned without the aid of water. Choke on stale air too jagged to release from your bronchial tubes. But I remained too fatigued to scream such obscenities, to find out if I was destined for the same.

In the end, our vision diluted. A mass cultivated inside your brainstem. You tried to asphyxiate yourself with whatever you could find. Which, only provided a temporary comfort, as your body was engulfed with no motivation at all to be alive. I know you questioned it more than a thousand times. It's hard to find meaning without blood, I understand.

The last time I saw you, I couldn't feel my eyes. They were too burnt from the condensation. I didn't expect you to find me. Normally, my face flushed with blood surging to the surface with just the thought of you, but on that day I knew I was drained. Tapped out. And that's when I knew our time had passed many moons ago. Shame, really, to feel so much and then nothing at all. But there was only so much someone could take before they have to decide between life and death. Frankly, you weren't worth it. Not sure you ever were.

So, do not blame me for taking pleasure from the irony as you inflicted much more pain upon yourself than I could have ever conjured. You needed no help in the path of destruction. You submerged me so deep below the surface I couldn't have helped you if I wanted. Any blood you had remaining, you plunged out on your own. But I was there, watching, waiting for my reemergence because I did not go away. I died, burying my body deep inside the folds of your gray matter.

What do you mean?
My face works fine.
The sagging skin,
it's a natural reaction
to the proceedings of life,
as we all eventually start
to drip from decomposition.
It's just that mine was expedited,
all thanks to you.

early morning risings,
witching hours,
hunting for answers,
dispelled from reason,
watching network shows,
shaking in a plague
of exhaustion.

I've felt nothing for days,
numb and glitching.
So, I boiled water
to drain it away,
scald my skin,
to evaluate a nerve defect
that inhibits sensation.
Otherwise, I may fall
into a daze
that could
rupture vessels
in my brain
and
destroy me.

dreaming nostalgia,
cool breeze,
shudder and shiver,
the stench of horror
lingers under hair
to endure
what breeds.

The thing about phantoms,
they never disappear.
Their figures move
in and out the spectrum of light,
utilizing your body
to weave in manipulation.
And in the dark,
they present a broadcast
exploiting the lack of electromagnetic radiation
by blanketing their presence in wavelengths.
It's to remind you
that even in the shelter of the night
there is nowhere to hide.

i hope you found
a good use
for the portion
of my soul
you stole
from me

pillow wrapped face
leaking from orifices
pumping out depravity
theatrical dormant instincts
jumping through electrical circuits

no shadows from boulders
lighted crossroads
obsolete pathways
caffeinated binges

Escape is improbable.

Self-induced desensitization,
all it takes is just one more.
No longer need to endure
an antagonized amygdala.
Man has resolved this dilemma
with synthetic dust.
Encapsulated.
All it takes is a swallow.

I laid sedated on the bathroom floor
praying I didn't take too much
while also praying I did
because I wanted it all to end
and it felt like my only way out.

i have found comfort
in many rooms
where profound,
visceral words spill,
pooling in a puddle
of perfumed affliction,
enough for my head
to submerge
into the multicollinearity
of neural networks,
but masking the vacancy
of the compartment
which is inhabited
only by myself.

I question my organs.
What drives their functionality
to have such a needless
pursuit of perpetual futility,
keeping a carcass alive,
digesting and breathing,
despite the rapid decay?

Today I punctured my chest,
I took a knife,
carved a hole
as I haven't felt the throb
and I needed verification.

Releasing it from its confines,
palpating in my hand,
spouting out blood,
I watched astonished
to find it in working order
once separated from its cage.

With teenage years passed,
I wake up as an adult,
cautious of rapport,
now schooled in sharp objects,
evident by my sliced arteries.

My skin pleads for platelets
to clot my wounds
but life continues on
with or without a pulse.

And my howls to the moon
would only go so far.

I use surgical glue
to appear undamaged,
an efficacious citizen,
but knowing the glue's inevitable dissolve
is heading my way.

So, I consume barrels of alcohol
as a substitute for blood
to keep the demon locked away.

# EXORCISM

The day you sought out a shaman to extract me from your intestines, I knew this would end in silence. No firework finale. The rage, despair went numb and I was stripped of much of my power as you were too. I did not fathom how hearing you utter my name would shatter the core of my existence. My reawakening became an exorcism.

I cannot fault you for this. I believe much of what happened sits stalely misunderstood. I lived a life without skin. I had hoped you would shed some for me to use, but you shed far too much. Now we both carry scar tissue and wear it as a shell. Part of me holds animosity for you, as I am sure a bitter taste remains in your mouth too. And the blame remains floating in the air.

Our relationship consisted of shadows and ghosts. Late night hopes followed by daytime nightmares. And I am grateful for an end as I thought I'd forever remain stuck within. Now we have time to allow for the anger and humility to dissipate as our bodies regenerate blood. I will always be able to smell yours as you will of mine but the scent has changed into a dim alert for the nervous system. It's nothing more than a memory that's no longer locked in storage and wrapped in barbwire.

Now, after extraction, I can sit out in the open without getting sunburned. Your hair lightens with the exposure, golden. And it's odd, our tale makes others uncomfortable, keeping a lingering shame. You see, there was damage in your procedure, your brainstem remains imperfect and raw, but overall you feel less pain. Together we are no more and healing begins.

The light, darkness, and blood were all metaphors of a perspective that took a long time to formulate. Stewed and cooked to tell a story that causes stomach aches, but with small sips, it does hurt less.

I've been howling at the moon
but I haven't heard back.

So, I called upon the stars
in a moment of desperation
to summon enough energy
to speak your name.

I can remember now,
why I've been shut down.

It's not my sensitivity
or my paralyzing shame.

You've used my damage
to confuse me of weakness,
but this remains about you
and your delusions.

I've only shaved
the tip of the iceberg,
much of what sinks me
remains submerged.
Yet, I lack some sharpness
in my appearance
which had often
frightened away the sun's rays.

Now, many beams
grace my frozen exterior,
softening the layers
I've used as a shield.
I had feared that melting
would ruin me
but in the light,
I can see how it loosens me
to be able to melt in with
what surrounds me.

if you need me
to be the villain
in your story then
so be it,

but allow me
to continue writing
my own tale.

Humorist realizations,
I found solace
in the company
of the same species
to discuss your actions.

it was a fragment
of my troubles
that blasted out of my skull,

but shrapnel still remains
inside other compartments
left undug due to the necessary courage
of getting the surgery
for an extraction.

yet, with this one container opened
it makes the room feel lighter,
a smidge less cramp,
enough space to take a seat,

for the entire surface of my buttock
to feel the ground
and anchor me down with roots.

You didn't care much to be ignored,
the uncertainty of my answers
drove you into an inferno
the more I ignored, the more fire raged.

It's as if you thought it was a game
requiring the grit of coal
and stamina to endure drowning waters.

But the delusion did not include flames
as I was nothing more than a girl
being forced to endure a blaze
ignited by an adult.

I still feel anxious under the fluorescent lights,
I still look over my shoulder in grocery stores,
I worry about every bustle in a bush.
I've developed heightened senses,
survival skills awarded to me for enduring the hunt.

So, I felt inclined to plaster layers of soot on my face,
but the layers hardened into a metal, shielding me
from major milestones, and teenage romances.
I busied myself, camouflaged in the woods,
not the giants, gnomes, or goblins could find me.

I walked paths leading to shameful fits,
purity of engagement, avoidant lies.
I mourned a life not lived through bursts of neglect,
and when I take several steps back,
I can see the destruction I caused myself.
No amount of hiding
could shake away the feelings of the hunt.

Yet, the criteria for my diagnosis
does not solely fall upon you.
You see, I lived in a house of silence,
where I cleaned up the midnight vomit,
where blood pooled in the bathroom.
And even through that, I could decipher
your taste for my blood was vile.

why write
about joy
when I
can harness
the power
of trauma
through the
written word.

# ABOUT THE AUTHOR

## Marie Casey

Marie is often found tip-tapping away on a keyboard or face deep in a book. In her past life, she was a timid, cave dwelling mouse. Now she seeks to experience sunlight in the dream of sharing her words with the flowers she has admired for years.

You can connect with Marie on Twitter @themariecasey or email at mariecaseywrites@gmail.com.

Printed in Great Britain
by Amazon